D1607262

MIRANDA RIGHTS

Protecting the Rights of the Accused

G. S. Prentzas

The Rosen Publishing Group, Inc., New York

To my parents, John and Marilyn

Published in 2006 by The Rosen Publishing Group, Inc.
29 East 21st Street, New York, NY 10010

Library of Congress Cataloging-in-Publication Data

Prentzas, G. S.
Miranda rights: protecting the rights of the accused/G. S. Prentzas.–1st ed.
    p. cm.–(The Library of American laws and legal principles)
Includes bibliographical references and index.
ISBN 1-4042-0454-7 (library binding)
1. Miranda, Ernesto–Trials, litigation, etc. 2. Trials (Rape)–Arizona. 3. Right to counsel–United States. 4. Self-incrimination–United States. 5. Confession (Law)–United States. 6. Police questioning–United States. I. Title. II. Series.
KF224.M54P74 2006
345.73'056–dc22

                                                                    2004030086

Manufactured in the United States of America

On the cover: The main entrance of the United States Supreme Court building faces the U.S. Capitol in Washington, D.C. The marble statue on the right side of the entrance represents Authority of Law and was carved by James Earle Fraser. The male figure holds a sword and a tablet, on which is written the Latin word *Lex*, meaning "law."

CONTENTS

INTRODUCTION

"You have the right to remain silent. If you give up the right to remain silent, anything you say can and will be used against you in a court of law. You have the right to an attorney. If you desire an attorney and cannot afford one, an attorney will be obtained for you before police questioning."

Anyone who has watched a TV police drama has heard this speech or one similar to it. Every day, police officers throughout the United States recite these words of warning to suspects before formally questioning them about specific crimes.

The "you have a right to remain silent" speech is known as the Miranda warning because its legal requirements were established in a groundbreaking 1966 U.S. Supreme Court case, *Miranda v. Arizona*. In that case, the Court ruled that statements made by a person accused of a crime could not be used as evidence at his or her trial unless the accused "voluntarily, knowingly, and intelligently" waived the constitutional right to remain silent. It was a revolutionary and highly controversial decision. Until that time, the right to remain silent had been thought to apply only to trials. The Fifth Amendment to the U.S. Constitution guaranteed criminal defendants the right not to testify against themselves in a court of law. In *Miranda*, however, the Supreme Court extended the right to remain silent beyond the courtroom to the police interrogation room.

The U.S. Supreme Court's decision had a major impact on law enforcement, creating a new procedure

A police officer in Texas reads a suspect his Miranda rights in 1996. The U.S. Supreme Court ruled in *Miranda v. Arizona* (1966) that before a suspect can be interrogated, police must inform the suspect that he or she has the rights to remain silent and to have a lawyer present during questioning.

for police officers to follow before questioning suspects or obtaining confessions. Since *Miranda*, the police have been required to inform suspects of their constitutional rights to remain silent and to have an attorney present before the police can begin their interrogation. The rights contained in the Miranda warning are often called Miranda rights, and when suspects have been read their rights, they are said to have been "Mirandized." The *Miranda* ruling also sparked a passionate debate on an important criminal justice issue: how can the U.S. legal system balance the government's duty to protect law-abiding citizens with the constitutional rights of the accused?

CHAPTER ONE

"You Have the Right to Remain Silent . . ."

On March 13, 1963, Officer Carroll Cooley and Detective Wilfred Young escorted a suspect into a Phoenix, Arizona, police station for questioning. Their investigation of a rape had led them to the doorstep of Ernesto Miranda, a twenty-three-year-old Mexican American who had been in trouble with the law since he was fourteen. Miranda had a prior arrest record for armed robbery, attempted rape, burglary, and assault. In the driveway of the house that Miranda shared with his girlfriend, the officers had discovered his girlfriend's car, which matched the rape victim's description of her attacker's vehicle.

The victim was an eighteen-year-old woman who was later identified in court papers as Lois Ann Jameson, although that was not her real name. She had been attacked as she returned home alone from her late-night job. Her assailant forced Jameson into a car at knifepoint, drove out into the Arizona desert, and sexually assaulted her. He took her money before dropping Jameson off a few blocks from her home. She later recalled the crime to detectives, describing her attacker as a Mexican man, probably in his late twenties, with a slight build. He was unshaven and wore glasses, jeans, and a T-shirt.

Ernesto Miranda used this car in March 1963 when he attacked a woman, known by the alias Lois Ann Jameson, in Phoenix, Arizona. Police officers were able to track down Miranda through Jameson's description of the old green car.

As they drove Miranda to the station house, Cooley and Young were convinced that they had solved the crime. They quickly placed Miranda in a lineup, along with three Mexican American men from the city jail. The four men looked somewhat similar, although Miranda was the only one wearing eyeglasses and a T-shirt, two items that the victim had stated her rapist had been wearing. Jameson told the officers that Miranda's features and build most resembled that of her attacker, but she couldn't say for sure that it was Miranda who had attacked her.

P.D. PHOENIX, ARIZ.
APPO NTED   PHOTO

Officer Carroll F. Cooley, the detective in charge of Jameson's case, arrested Miranda with fellow officer Wilfred Young on March 13, 1963. Miranda agreed to accompany the police to the Phoenix police station for questioning. Miranda asked why he was being arrested, but the officers said they could not tell him.

THE INTERROGATION

Cooley and Young led their suspect into an interrogation room. When Miranda asked about the outcome of the lineup, one of the officers intimated that he had flunked, even though Jameson had failed to make a positive identification. For the next two hours, the officers questioned their suspect. They would testify in court that they neither hurt nor threatened him. Although the detectives were aware that the U.S. Constitution gave Miranda the right to remain silent, the law did not require them to inform him of this right.

According to Liva Baker in *Miranda: Crime, Law, and Politics* (1985), Miranda claimed that Cooley and Young had tried to bully him during the interrogation, telling him "they would throw the book" at him—that is, they would make all possible charges against

PHOENIX PD
63 08380
3 13 63

Ernesto Miranda *(far left)* was put in a lineup with three other young Mexican Americans so that Jameson could try to identify the man who raped her. Miranda was the only suspect who wore eyeglasses and a T-shirt, items Jameson had stated were worn by her attacker.

him. Maintaining that he felt pressured by the detectives, Miranda said he soon confessed that he raped Jameson. The interrogation continued, and soon Miranda admitted that he committed eight other unsolved crimes in the area, including a robbery and an attempted rape. He would later contend that the detectives told him that the rape charge could be dropped if he confessed to one of the robberies. Cooley and Young later denied that they offered Miranda any deals.

The detectives asked Miranda to make a written confession of the Jameson rape. They handed him a standard police department form used for suspect statements. A typed paragraph at the top of the

Form 2000-66-D
Rev. Nov. 59

**CITY OF PHOENIX, ARIZONA
POLICE DEPARTMENT**

Witness/Suspect
Statement

SUBJECT: _Rape_ _D.R. 63-08380_

STATEMENT OF: _Ernest Arther Miranda_

TAKEN BY: _C. Cooley #413 - W. Young #182_

DATE: _3-13-63_ TIME: _(1:30) Pm_ PLACE TAKEN: _Interr Rm #2_

I, _Ernest A. Miranda_, do hereby swear that I make this statement voluntarily and of my own free will, with no threats, coercion, or promises of immunity, and with full knowledge of my legal rights, understanding any statement I make may be used against me.

I, _Ernest A. Miranda_, am _23_ years of age and have completed the _8th_ grade in school.

Seen a girl walking up street stopped a little ahead of her got out of car walked towards her grabbed her by the arm and asked to get in the car. Got in car without force tied hands + ankles. Drove away for a few miles. Stopped asked to take clothes off. Did not, asked me to take her back home I started to take clothes off her without any force. and with cooperation. Asked her to lay down and she did. Could not get penis into vagina got about ½ (half) inch in. Told her to get clothes back on. Drove her home. I couldn't say I was sorry for what I have done. But asked her to say a prayer for me.

I have read and understand the foregoing statement and hereby swear to its truthfulness.

WITNESS: _Carroll Cooley_ _Ernest A. Miranda._
Wilford M. Young #182

Miranda wrote this confession on March 13, 1963, after being interrogated by officers Cooley and Young. Even though Jameson had not positively identified Miranda during the lineup, the officers had intimated that she had pointed him out as having attacked her. The officers did not tell Miranda that he had the right to remain silent and to have an attorney at his side during their questioning. After about two hours of interrogation, Miranda broke down and confessed to the crime.

form stated that the confession was made voluntarily, without threats or promises of immunity, and "with full knowledge of my legal rights, understanding any statement I make may be used against me." The form did not explain exactly what Miranda's "legal rights" were. In his written confession, Miranda described the rape, and his version matched the victim's account in many respects. He signed his name at the bottom, underneath a typed sentence stating, "I have read and understand the foregoing statement and hereby swear to its truthfulness." The two officers signed the document as witnesses.

Miranda was transferred to the city jail in Phoenix. Two days later, he was formally charged with the kidnapping and rape of Lois Ann Jameson. Because Miranda had no money to pay for legal counsel, the court assigned him a lawyer, Alvin Moore. The experienced seventy-three-year-old attorney felt that it would be extremely difficult to convince a jury of his client's innocence because Miranda had confessed to the crimes in writing.

TRIAL AND APPEAL

On June 20, 1963, Miranda's trial for kidnapping and raping Lois Ann Jameson began. Prosecutors (the attorneys representing the state of Arizona) called four people to testify against Miranda: Jameson, her sister, Officer Cooley, and Detective Young. On the witness stand, Jameson described her abduction and rape. Cooley and Young testified about their investigation of the crime and their questioning of the defendant. The prosecution submitted only one document into evidence: Miranda's written confession. In his defense of Miranda, Alvin Moore offered no witnesses. He focused instead on the cross-examination of the victim and the arresting officers.

The jury considered the evidence for five hours before returning to the courtroom with their verdict: they found the defendant guilty of kidnapping and raping Jameson. On June 27, 1963, the judge sentenced Miranda to serve twenty to thirty years in state prison.

Although the jury had found Miranda guilty, his attorney believed that he could still win the case. Moore appealed the verdict to the Arizona Supreme Court, arguing that his client had been denied a fair trial because it was just as important for a defendant to have legal counsel during police questioning as it was during trial. Moore argued that Miranda would not have confessed if a lawyer had been there to advise him of his right to remain silent. The Arizona Supreme Court upheld Miranda's conviction, ruling that the police had not violated his constitutional rights in obtaining the confession. The Arizona Supreme Court concluded that because Miranda had *voluntarily* confessed to the crimes, the prosecutor was allowed to present the confession to the jury.

Miranda continued to fight his conviction. Without the assistance of a lawyer, he filed an appeal directly to the nation's highest court: the Supreme Court of the United States. Two prominent Phoenix attorneys, John J. Flynn and John P. Frank, agreed to handle Miranda's appeal pro bono, or free of charge. In the preceding two years, the U.S. Supreme Court had expanded the rights of the accused in well-publicized cases, such as *Gideon v. Wainright* and *Escobedo v. Illinois.* Miranda's attorneys felt that their client's case presented an important constitutional issue that the Court should address. In November 1965, the attorneys told Miranda that the Supreme Court had agreed to review his case.

MIRANDA V. ARIZONA

The U.S. Supreme Court considered *Miranda v. Arizona* along with three other cases involving defendants who had been questioned by police without the presence of an attorney. On June 13, 1966, the Supreme Court announced its decision in *Miranda* and the other three cases. Because the issues presented by these cases were so important, Chief Justice Earl Warren read the Court's majority decision, all sixty pages. By a narrow 5–4 vote, the U.S. Supreme Court ruled that the

When the U.S. Supreme Court ruled on the *Miranda* case, the Court decided that Miranda deserved a new trial. The Court ruled that Miranda's Fifth Amendment right to remain silent had been violated. Miranda *(right)* is seen here in 1967, with his lawyer John J. Flynn during his new trial.

use of the defendants' confessions as evidence had violated their Fifth Amendment right to remain silent. Justices Hugo L. Black, William O. Douglas, William J. Brennan, and Abe Fortas joined Earl Warren to form the majority in *Miranda*. The four dissenting justices were Potter Stewart, Tom C. Clark, John M. Harlan, and Byron R. White. The Court ordered new trials for Miranda and the other defendants.

Four of the Supreme Court justices fervently disagreed with the majority opinion, pointing out that each defendant had voluntarily confessed to his crimes. They further warned that the presence of lawyers in the interrogation room would "discourage any confession at all." Three of the dissenting justices stated that the decision had

13

"All the News That's Fit to Print"

The New York Times.

LATE CITY EDITION
U.S. Weather Bureau Report (Page 93) Forecast:
Mostly sunny, warm and humid today, tonight and tomorrow.
Temp. Range: 86—65; yesterday: 74—58.
Temp.-Hum. Index: about 72; yesterday 70.

VOL. CXV. No. 39,588.   NEW YORK, TUESDAY, JUNE 14, 1966.   TEN CENTS

LINDSAY REPORTS ALBANY PROGRESS ON CITY TAX PLAN

Mayor, Governor and High Local and State Officials Hold 11-Hour Session

STAFFS CONTINUE TALKS

Principals Will Meet Again Today—Budget Deadline for Council Is Friday

By RICHARD L. MADDEN
Special to The New York Times

ALBANY, June 13 — Top state and city officials were reported to have made progress tonight in their efforts to break the legislative impasse over a tax program for New York City.

Governor Rockefeller, Mayor Lindsay, legislative leaders and other state and city officials started their negotiations this morning and worked into the night in the seclusion of the Victorian, red-brick Executive Mansion five blocks from the Capitol.

Shortly after 10:30 P.M., Leslie Slote, the Governor's press secretary, told reporters waiting at the mansion's iron gate that progress had been made. But he refused to elaborate.

At stake in the talks was the question whether Mayor Lindsay would get the city income tax that he wants and whether upstate legislators would be successful in pressing their demands for an increase in the city transit fare and real estate tax.

Proposals Reviewed

Mr. Slote said that the Mayor, Governor and other leaders had left for the night and would resume their negotiations at 9 A.M. tomorrow.

Their staffs, he added, would continue working tonight. This was viewed as an indication that they might have some new proposals under consideration.

"We're making some progress," Mr. Lindsay said as he left the mansion after the 11-hour session. "I've learned never to be unhappy. Anyone you're making some progress there's hope."

Assembly Speaker Anthony J. Travia, Democrat of Brooklyn, said the discussions had focused on ways to close the city's revenue gap, which he estimated at "around $420-million." This was about the same amount of taxing power

Continued on Page 34, Column 1

BRYDGES MAY BOW ON THE CONDON ACT

Likely to Accept Rivals' Bid If Compromise Bid Fails

By SYDNEY H. SCHANBERG
Special to The New York Times

ALBANY, June 13 — The Legislature's top Republican has decided that if no compromise

DISCUSS CITY TAXES: At Albany meeting yesterday, from left: City Council President Frank D. O'Connor, Mayor Lindsay, Governor Rockefeller, Senate Majority Leader Earl W. Brydges and Assembly Speaker Anthony J. Travia. Mr. Brydges is Republican from Niagara Falls. Mr. Travia is a Brooklyn Democrat. Governor was host.

French Plan to Withdraw Some Air Units in Germany

By THOMAS J. HAMILTON
Special to The New York Times

BONN, June 13 — France informed West Germany today that she intended to move some or all of her aviation units out of this country after French ground and air units are withdrawn from the Atlantic alliance's command on July 1.

Reliable sources said that France had not specified when the aviation units would be returned to France or whether all of her 10,000 airmen in West Germany, stationed mostly at Lahr and Bremgarten, would be withdrawn. A Foreign Ministry spokesman said in Paris that for the time being only a small number would move back across the Rhine.

According to reliable information, Jacques de Beaumarchais, political director of the Foreign Ministry, announced the impending withdrawal at the start of a talk with Dr. Hermann Mayer-Lindenberg, the West German Foreign Minister's expert on the affairs of the North Atlantic Treaty Organization.

Although only local offices were at stake, the campaign was fought mainly on party ideological lines and with reference to national issues. This made it an important test of the popularity of the center-left Democratic Premier, Aldo Moro, and the four coalition parties—the Christian Democrats, Socialists, Democratic Socialists and Republicans.

In Rome Province, the center of the Communist drive to replace the Christian Democrats as the biggest party, the Communist vote appeared to have gained just short of 4 per cent. The center-left parties together had gained 9 per cent in the popular vote.

ITALIAN COALITION BOLSTERED IN VOTE

Cut in Communist Strength Emerges in Early Returns From Local Elections

By ROBERT C. DOTY
Special to The New York Times

ROME, Tuesday, June 14 — Early returns from municipal and provincial Italy indicated today that the governing coalition of center-left parties had reinforced its position and cut the Communist vote slightly.

Although only local offices were at stake, the campaign was fought mainly on party ideological lines and with reference to national issues.

Premier's Party Gains

In the same areas, the Christian Democrats appeared to have gained just short of 4 per cent.

Returns from Rome's municipal elections lagged strangely. But if the city pattern followed that for the city and province combined, the center-left parties

2 SAIGON MARCHES HALTED BY POLICE

Buddhists Burn 2 Jeeps as 2d Effort to Deliver Letter to U.S. Embassy Fails

By NEIL SHEEHAN
Special to The New York Times

SAIGON, South Vietnam, Tuesday, June 14 — A crowd of about 500 Buddhist demonstrators burned two jeeps, one a United States military vehicle, this morning after riot policemen had turned back their attempt to march on the United States Embassy.

Three American servicemen in the jeep escaped unhurt but abandoned a submachine gun, which was seized by the demonstrators. The other jeep was a South Vietnamese police vehicle and its occupants were also believed to have escaped unharmed.

The demonstrators included monks in yellow robes, nuns and youths. They attempted a similar march on the embassy yesterday but were driven back by tear-gas grenades.

The object of the protest was to present to embassy officials a box containing United States-made tear-gas grenades as an ironical gift for President Johnson. The grenades had been hurled by Government policemen seeking to break up earlier Buddhist demonstrations.

Carrying Letter to Johnson

The crowd was also carrying a copy of a letter to Mr. Johnson from Thich Tam Chau, a vice chairman of the Secular Affairs Institute of the Unified Buddhist Church.

The letter accused Mr. Johnson of having turned "deaf ears to our cries for human decency and human rights."

"Please do not make yourself so unpopular and a victim of hatred by supporting this cruel, military and inefficient regime," the letter said in a reference to the ruling military junta.

The Buddhists have invited the Embassy to send a representative to receive the box of

Continued on Page 2, Column 2

Kosygin, in Finland, Urges All Nations Aid Vietnam Peace

By PETER GROSE
Special to The New York Times

HELSINKI, Finland, June 13 — Premier Aleksei N. Kosygin called today for more active efforts by all nations to bring peace in Vietnam.

In the first statement of his six-day official visit to Finland, the Soviet Premier's restraint in speaking of Vietnam was even more marked than in a speech last week, when he first set this new tone of moderation.

He said he regretted that "armed aggression is being committed against the people of Vietnam." But he did not point to the United States as an aggressor, although that has been a standard theme of Soviet foreign policy declarations.

Struggle for Peace Urged

"In the age of rockets and nuclear technology, nations and governments cannot simply hope for peace, but must actively struggle for peace," the Soviet Premier said.

"A broad front of all those for whom international security is deep must join in this struggle."

Mr. Kosygin spoke at a banquet in the Presidential Palace, residence of President Urho K. Kekkonen.

The Soviet Premier, accompanied by his blonde wife, Klavdiya, arrived by overnight train from Moscow this afternoon. It is his first visit as Premier to a non-Communist European country.

Mr. Kekkonen, who spoke before Mr. Kosygin at the banquet, made no mention of Vietnam though he stressed that Finland's policy of neutrality "does not mean passive unconcern and isolation."

It was for Mr. Kosygin to pinpoint the topics he expected to discuss with the Finnish leaders. He expressed Soviet interest in reviving efforts toward reaching a "reliable collective security system" for Europe.

"The security of Europe depends, in our opinion, above all on the European states themselves

Continued on Page 2, Column 3

HIGH COURT PUTS NEW CURB ON POWERS OF THE POLICE TO INTERROGATE SUSPECTS

Law on Puerto Rican Vote Upheld by Supreme Court

7-2 Ruling Declares Literacy in Spanish Meets State Test—Dissenters Fear Widening of Congressional Power

By WARREN WEAVER Jr.
Special to The New York Times

WASHINGTON, June 13 — The 1965 Federal law permitting thousands of Puerto Ricans to vote in New York on the basis of Spanish literacy was upheld today by the United States Supreme Court.

The 7-to-2 decision reversed a ruling by a three-judge Federal Court last November that the controversial section of the

Excerpts from Court opinions appear on Page 26.

Voting Rights Act of 1965 interfered improperly with a state's right to set its own voting standards.

Justice William J. Brennan Jr., who wrote the majority opinion on voting by Puerto Ricans are "appropriate legislation" to enforce the 14th

Continued on Page 26, Column 4

Amendment to the Constitution.

That amendment forbids the states to adopt any law that would "deny to any person within its jurisdiction the equal protection of the laws."

Until Congress acted last year, New York State had required literacy in English, or a sixth-grade education in an English-speaking school, as condition of voting. Under the law upheld today, persons with a sixth-grade education from a Puerto Rican school in which Spanish is the principal language also have the right to vote.

The principal effect of this literacy section of the Voting Rights Act of 1965 and of today's decision is in New York City, where about 750,000 Puerto Ricans live.

When the Spanish literacy

Continued on Page 26, Column 4

7 Shot in New Chicago Riot As Settlement Efforts Fail

By DONALD JANSON
Special to The New York Times

CHICAGO, June 13 — Violence flared again tonight in Chicago's principal Puerto Rican neighborhood. Rock-tossing youths ran through the community on the Northwest Side, smashing car and store windows and traffic lights, tipping over mailboxes, stealing merchandise and harassing police cars.

By the time the police had restored order, seven persons had been shot and several others had been injured and others badly enough to require hospital treatment.

It was the second night of rioting on Division Street. The waves of violence followed the shooting yesterday of a Puerto Rican youth by a patrolman.

Last night gangs burned two squad cars, damaged a third and went on a window-smashing rampage. Before calm was restored, 16 persons had been injured and 49 arrested.

Tonight Puerto Rican community leaders suggested that the police leave peace efforts to them. Marked police cars were withdrawn from Division Street. Then 1,200 persons turned out for a rally in the area's Humboldt Park. Some of the speakers renewed charges of police brutality.

A second night of rioting followed. The police moved back onto Division Street in force, dispersing the crowds with

Continued on Page 18, Column 3

SENTENCING DEALS IN STATE BARRED

U.S. Judge Rules Leniency May Not Be Promised to Induce Guilty Pleas

By EDWARD RANZAL

Judge Edward Weinfeld of the Federal District Court ruled yesterday that judges in state courts could not promise lenient prison terms to defendants to induce them to plead guilty.

Striking for the first time at a very sensitive area in legal procedure, the judge declared that this "fairly common" practice in state courts deprived a defendant of his constitutional right of due process.

On the basis of Judge Weinfeld's 20-page opinion, it is expected that many state prisoners serving sentences based on promises made by the sentencing judge will move to Federal court to have their convictions set aside. However, they will face the possibility that a long-

DISSENTERS BITTER

Four View Limitation on Confessions as Aid to Criminals

Excerpts from Court opinions are printed on Page 24.

By FRED P. GRAHAM
Special to The New York Times

WASHINGTON, June 13 — The Supreme Court announced today sweeping limitations on the power of the police to question suspects in their custody.

The justices split 5 to 4. In stinging dissents the minority denounced the decision as helping criminals go free to repeat their crimes.

The majority opinion, by Chief Justice Earl Warren, broke new constitutional ground by declaring that the Fifth Amendment's privilege against self-incrimination comes into play as soon as a person is within police custody.

Consequently, under the ruling, the prosecution cannot use in a trial any admissions or confessions made by the suspect while in custody unless it first proves that the police complied with a detailed list of safeguards to protect the right against self-incrimination.

The suspect, the Court said, must have been clearly warned that he may remain silent, that anything he says may be held against him and that he has a right to have a lawyer present during interrogation.

Court-Appointed Counsel

If the suspect desires a lawyer but cannot afford one, he cannot be questioned unless a court-appointed lawyer is present.

If the suspect confesses after receiving the required warnings, the burden is on the prosecution to prove a knowing waiver of rights. And any prolonged interrogation will be taken to show a lack of waiver.

Moreover, the majority opinion said, if the suspect makes a knowing waiver but later asks to see a lawyer, all questioning must stop until he sees one. If the suspect is alone and starts to talk, but then indicates "in any manner" that he wants to remain silent, the police must stop questioning him.

Ruling Called 'Dangerous'

Although Chief Justice Warren stressed that the ruling did not outlaw confessions, the majority's opinion drew bitter dissenting remarks from Justices Tom C. Clark, John M. Harlan, Potter Stewart and Byron R. White.

Justice Harlan, his face flushed and his voice occasionally faltering with emotion, denounced the decision as "dangerous experimentation" at a

---

The front page of the *New York Times* on June 14, 1966, a day after the Court made its decision on *Miranda v. Arizona,* had the headline "High Court Puts New Curb on Powers of the Police to Interrogate Suspects." In the article, reporter Fred P. Graham wrote, "Under the ruling, the prosecution cannot use in a trial any admissions or confessions made by the suspect while in custody unless it first proves that the police complied with a detailed list of safeguards to protect the right against self-incrimination."

The Fate of Ernesto Miranda

Ernesto Miranda faced a new trial on the rape and kidnapping charges in 1967, and this time the prosecutor could not use his confession. It appeared that Miranda would avoid conviction in his second trial until his former girlfriend, Twila Hoffman, testified that Miranda had also confessed to the rape to her, three days after his written confession to the police. The jury found Miranda guilty, and he received the same sentence he had been given four years earlier, twenty to thirty years in prison. He was paroled (released early) in 1974 and died two years later after being stabbed over a card game in a barroom brawl with two men. Miranda's killer escaped, but the Phoenix police arrested the second man. As the police drove the suspect to the police station, one of the officers read him the Miranda rights.

little support in previous court decisions and required "a strained reading of [the] history" of the Fifth Amendment.

In *Miranda*, the Court provided guidelines for police interrogations. Prior to questioning suspects, police officers had to inform them of the following:

1. That they had the right to remain silent
2. That anything they said could be used against them in a court of law
3. That they had the right to the presence of an attorney to assist them
4. That if they could not afford an attorney, one would be appointed prior to any questioning

A suspect could waive, or give up, any of these rights, as long as it was a voluntary decision. Once a suspect stated that he or she understood his or her Miranda rights and waived them, any statement the suspect made would generally be admissible in court. The Court also stressed that this four-part warning was a minimum: the U.S. Congress and the states could find other remedies to protect the rights of the accused.

As a result of the *Miranda* decision, police investigators were required to notify suspects of their rights to remain silent and to have legal counsel before questioning. Notification of these rights had to be made at the moment the person could reasonably be considered a suspect under interrogation, even if that moment came before an arrest. If at any stage in the interrogation a detained suspect indicated that he or she wanted to consult with a lawyer, the questioning must stop. If the person declined to be interrogated, the questioning must stop. Any evidence gained in violation of *Miranda* would be inadmissible at a trial.

CHAPTER TWO
Rights of the Accused

The Supreme Court's landmark decision in 1966 in *Miranda v. Arizona* was, at the time, the latest development in the broadening of rights granted to Americans accused of crimes. Many of the U.S. legal system's basic laws and procedures can be traced to Great Britain. Parliament, Britain's legislative body, passed most of the laws that governed that empire's thirteen colonies in North America. Courts in the thirteen colonies applied British laws and followed the criminal procedures of the British legal system that governed the British Empire. In Britain, the right to a trial by a jury of one's peers had long been granted to criminal defendants. In 1215, King John (1167–1216) had signed the Magna Carta, a document that limited the powers of the British monarchy. In addition to addressing the complaints of the British nobility, it set down the basic legal rights of all of the country's free men. (The document did not address the rights of women; in thirteenth-century British law, husbands and fathers controlled the legal affairs of their wives and daughters under the doctrine of coverture.) Notably, the Magna Carta forbade taxation without representation and guaranteed the right to a trial by jury.

The Magna Carta (the Great Charter) is sometimes called King John's Charter of Liberties. An original copy of the document from 1215 is pictured here. The Magna Carta is often considered to be the chief defense against arbitrary and unjust rule in Britain. Although the original Magna Carta was issued in 1215, it was reissued several times later to give additional freedoms to the British people. In America, the Founding Fathers relied on many of the rights affirmed in the Magna Carta when they wrote the Declaration of Independence, acclaiming their rightful liberties from George III and the British parliament.

CONSTITUTIONAL SAFEGUARDS

Political and economic grievances in the British colonies led to the American Revolution (1775–1783). After winning the war and securing their independence from Britain, the thirteen states approved the Articles of Confederation, the United States' first national constitution, in 1781. Because of their experience with central authority under British rule, most Americans wanted governmental power to stay

The Bill of Rights

The seven articles of the U.S. Constitution spelled out the powers of the federal government, but it did not make clear the ways in which the federal government could not act. Several states' delegates during the Constitutional Convention objected that the proposed Constitution failed to protect individual liberties and threatened not to ratify it unless it guaranteed basic civil rights. Virginia's Thomas Jefferson argued, "A bill of rights is what the people are entitled to against every government on earth, general or particular, and what no just government should refuse, or rest on inference." To ensure that the Constitution would be ratified, the delegates at the Constitutional Convention agreed that a bill of rights would be added to the document. Ratified on December 15, 1791, the Bill of Rights consists of the first ten amendments to the Constitution. These amendments guarantee the basic civil rights of all U.S. citizens, including freedom of speech, freedom of the press, and freedom of religion.

In 1856, Junius Brutus Stearns painted *Washington as Statesman at the Constitutional Convention*. The first ten amendments to the Constitution are called the Bill of Rights. The Bill of Rights was added to the Constitution as a condition for ratification by the states on the insistence of the convention delegates who had doubts about a strong central government.

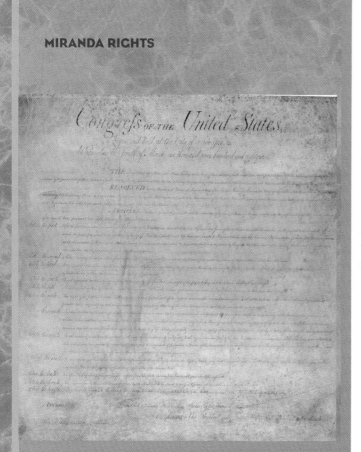

The Bill of Rights became a part of the U.S. Constitution in 1791. The Fifth and Sixth Amendments protect the rights of people accused of committing crimes. Over the years, amendments have been added one by one. As of 2005, there were twenty-seven amendments to the Constitution, the last one having been adopted in 1992.

mostly with the states. As a result, the Articles of Confederation created a weak national government, which eventually led to major disputes between the states. In 1787, delegates from the states met in Philadelphia, Pennsylvania, to improve the Articles of Confederation. The delegates, however, proposed that the nation's central government be completely reorganized. They drafted the U.S. Constitution, which established a republican form of government, with legislative, judicial, and executive branches. The legislative branch (Congress) would enact laws; the judicial branch (the courts) would interpret and apply the laws; and the executive branch (the president and other federal departments) would enforce the laws. When it went into effect in 1789, the Constitution provided the fundamental law of the United States.

Two years after the Constitution was ratified, ten amendments, known as the Bill of Rights, were added to guarantee individual liberties. The colonists' conflicts with British authority had broadened the American sense of liberty, and these ten amendments reflected the new nation's commitment to civil rights and justice. At first, the Bill of Rights applied only to the federal government, however. Many states adopted similar provisions in their own constitutions, but the rights granted to citizens and the judicial interpretations of these rights varied greatly among the states. Nevertheless, since the passage of the Fourteenth Amendment in 1868, after the Civil War, the states have also become responsible for upholding many of the rights and liberties contained in the Bill of Rights. The Fourteenth Amendment was designed primarily to make former slaves citizens of the United States and the states in which they lived. States were not allowed to "deprive any person of life, liberty, or property, without due process of law." Later Supreme Court decisions interpreted the Fourteenth Amendment to mean that states could not deny constitutional rights to any of their citizens.

The Bill of Rights proclaimed many safeguards to protect the rights of the accused. A defendant must receive fair notice of the charges, and excessive bail cannot be used to keep a defendant in custody. A defendant is entitled to a speedy trial. Criminal trials must be public and tried by an impartial jury. Defendants have the right to confront and cross-examine witnesses. Evidence gathered illegally, either by an unreasonable search of a defendant or his or her property or by an unreasonable seizure of his or her papers or effects, cannot be used against a defendant. A person cannot twice be tried for the same offense (known as double jeopardy), and punishment of those found guilty cannot be excessive or cruel.

Two additional safeguards provided by the Bill of Rights played important roles in the Supreme Court's decision in *Miranda v. Arizona*: freedom from self-incrimination and the right to counsel.

Self-Incrimination

The Fifth Amendment forbids the federal government from making a person "in any criminal case to be a witness against himself." Based on this amendment, the Supreme Court first prohibited use of involuntary confessions in *Brown v. Mississippi* (1936). In later cases, it outlawed many brutal methods used by police to pressure suspects into confessing. It prohibited interrogations that used torture or any other incentives, such as threats of future punishment and promises of leniency. To ensure that confessions were intentional and reliable, evidence obtained through coercion, or force, could not be presented to a jury. By 1959, the Court had ruled (in *Spano v. New York*) that confessions obtained by psychological ploys and trickery were inadmissible as evidence.

To determine whether a confession was admissible as evidence, courts focused on whether the confession had been voluntary. They looked carefully at the circumstances of the interrogation: where and when it took place, the characteristics of the suspect (age, education, and criminal background), and the specific actions of the police. Departure from normal procedures, such as delays in charging the suspect or holding him or her for long periods of time without allowing the suspect to speak with family, friends, or legal counsel, sometimes led courts to determine that a confession had not been voluntary. In many trials, deciding whether a defendant's confession had been voluntary proved difficult, and cases often boiled down to whether the court believed the defendant's or the police's account of the interrogation process.

The Right to Counsel

One of the most basic principles in American criminal law is that a person who is charged with a crime should have a fair trial. The framers of the Bill of Rights included in the Sixth Amendment a provision that guarantees to citizens accused "in all criminal prosecutions" the "right to assistance of counsel" for their defense. States, however, made their own rules on legal representation in cases involving state criminal laws. In *Powell v. Alabama* (1936), the U.S. Supreme Court made it clear that the assistance of counsel was a fundamental ingredient in any fair trial, federal or state,

Danny Escobedo is pictured here in 1966. While he was being questioned by police during a murder investigation, Escobedo asked to see his lawyer. The lawyer had come to the station to help Escobedo, but the police refused to allow him into the interrogation room because they hoped to get Escobedo to confess to the crime. Escobedo confessed, was tried, and because of statements he had made during the interrogation, he was convicted and sentenced to twenty years in prison. In *Escobedo v. Illinois* (1964), the U.S. Supreme Court overturned Escobedo's conviction and ruled that a suspect has a right to a lawyer during interrogation.

involving the death penalty. In later cases, the Supreme Court held that although assistance of counsel wasn't necessary in every state criminal trial, it was essential if "special circumstances" existed. The presence of these special circumstances would be determined on a case-by-case basis. The Supreme Court eventually abandoned its unclear special-circumstances rule, however. In *Gideon v. Wainright* (1963), the Court unanimously ordered a new trial for a defendant who had been denied a court-appointed lawyer to represent him in his burglary trial. The *Gideon* ruling made the Sixth Amendment's guarantee of the right to counsel mandatory in all state felony cases, such as those involving robbery, murder, and other major crimes.

One year later, the Court considered a case that made clearer at which stage in the criminal process a suspect is entitled to counsel. During an interrogation, the police had denied a defendant's repeated requests to consult his lawyer. Statements that the defendant eventually made were used against him in his murder trial. In *Escobedo v. Illinois* (1964), the Court overturned the defendant's conviction, stressing the need for counsel when the police action shifts from a criminal investigation to a criminal accusation. In other words, the right to counsel goes into effect once the police have focused their investigation on an individual and the purpose of their investigation is to get a confession from that person. *Escobedo* extended the right to counsel from the trial stage to the interrogation level.

MIRANDA AND THE RIGHTS OF THE ACCUSED

Escobedo left police unsure about what procedures they should follow in questioning a suspect. The Court's decision in *Miranda* clarified two important issues. First, it reaffirmed the Court's decision in *Escobedo* that the Sixth Amendment right to counsel applied to police interrogations. Second, it extended the Fifth Amendment right to remain silent to the interrogation stage. At the time *Escobedo* and *Miranda* were decided, physical intimidation and psychological pressure were common during police interrogations. To increase the certainty that a defendant's confession had been voluntary, *Miranda* introduced a new procedure of notifying all suspects of their rights before police questioning could begin. The Court's decision would have a significant impact on the U.S. criminal justice system.

CHAPTER THREE
The Impact of *Miranda*

When the U.S. Supreme Court announced its ruling in *Miranda v. Arizona*, law enforcement officials and prosecutors nationwide reacted strongly. They criticized the decision, saying that the Miranda warnings would hurt criminal investigations and trials. They warned that informing suspects of their right against self-incrimination and their right to have an attorney present for police interrogations would make confessions nearly impossible to obtain. Law enforcement officials put a lot of effort into persuading suspects to confess because confessions are convincing evidence to present to juries. Because Miranda warnings would lead to fewer confessions, law enforcement officials predicted that conviction rates would drop dramatically and more criminals would be left on the streets to commit crimes.

At the time *Miranda* was decided, the United States was experiencing a significant increase in major crimes. Many people during the 1960s felt that the Court was holding back the police and overprotecting criminals. Some politicians also raised their voices against *Miranda*. In his 1968 presidential campaign, Richard Nixon, who had practiced law in New York City before his presidential run, voiced his disagreement with the *Miranda* decision. He said that the Supreme Court was more concerned with safeguarding criminals

On June 23, 1969, after Warren Burger *(right)* was sworn in as chief justice, President Richard M. Nixon *(center)* posed for photographs with Burger and former chief justice Earl Warren. Nixon had made good on a 1968 presidential campaign promise. Nixon said he would replace Chief Justice Earl Warren, who was close to retirement at that time, with a chief justice who would support legal procedures that would not unfairly limit the powers of law enforcement.

than law-abiding citizens. If elected, Nixon promised to replace Warren, whose retirement was imminent, with a chief justice who supported criminal procedure rules that did not unfairly restrain law enforcement. *Miranda* also displeased many members of the U.S. Congress. To limit the Court's ruling, Congress passed the Omnibus Crime and Control and Safe Streets Act of 1968. This act made voluntary statements or confessions given by suspects within six hours after their arrest admissible in federal criminal cases, even if the arrestees had not been informed of their Miranda rights.

EFFECT ON POLICE

To comply with the Supreme Court's new order to protect the constitutional rights of suspects, arresting officers began to recite

The nine Supreme Court justices who decided the *Miranda v. Arizona* case in 1966 were, from left to right: *(seated)* Justice Tom C. Clark, Justice Hugo L. Black, Chief Justice Earl Warren, Justice William O. Douglas, Justice John M. Harlan; *(standing)* Justice Byron R. White, Justice William J. Brennan Jr., Justice Potter Stewart, and Justice Abe Fortas. By a 5–4 vote, the justices ruled that the use of the defendants' confessions as evidence violated their right to remain silent.

the Miranda warning, as it became known, before conducting interrogations. Police departments printed cards containing the language that the local police departments wanted officers to use in advising suspects of their rights. A typical Miranda warning read as follows:

> *You have the right to remain silent. If you give up the right to remain silent, anything you say can and will be used against you in a court of law. You have the right to an attorney. If you desire an attorney and cannot afford one, an attorney will be obtained for you before police questioning.*

YOU HAVE THE RIGHT TO REMAIN SILENT.

ANYTHING YOU SAY CAN BE USED AGAINST YOU IN A COURT OF LAW.

YOU HAVE THE RIGHT TO THE PRESENCE OF AN ATTORNEY TO ASSIST YOU PRIOR TO QUESTIONING, AND TO BE WITH YOU DURING QUESTIONING, IF YOU SO DESIRE.

IF YOU CANNOT AFFORD AN ATTORNEY YOU HAVE THE RIGHT TO HAVE AN ATTORNEY APPOINTED FOR YOU PRIOR TO QUESTIONING.

DO YOU UNDERSTAND THESE RIGHTS?

WILL YOU VOLUNTARILY ANSWER MY QUESTIONS?

Ernesto A. Miranda 6-13-66

This card is an original Miranda rights card, which police officers carried to use as a reference until they had memorized the Miranda rights. The card was autographed by Ernesto Miranda, who also noted the date, June 13, 1966, the day the Court decided his case.

If a law enforcement officer fails to give a suspect the Miranda warning before questioning begins, or if the officer continues to question a suspect who asks to speak with an attorney, statements made by the suspect generally cannot be used against him or her.

An officer can arrest a suspect without reciting the Miranda warning. The suspect must be Mirandized, however, before the police can begin their interrogation. The Miranda warning also does not apply to basic police questions, such as asking suspects for their name and address. Also, a Miranda warning is not necessary when a criminal approaches authorities to confess a crime. It's also unnecessary when a person makes a spur-of-the-moment statement before police

Lineups and the Right to Counsel

After broadening the Sixth Amendment guarantee of the right to counsel to include the interrogation stage in *Escobedo* and *Miranda*, the Supreme Court under Earl Warren extended the right to counsel even further. In *United States v. Wade* and *Gilbert v. California*, two cases decided on the same day in 1968, the Court held that the right of counsel must be provided during the traditional lineup procedure used to identify suspects. Four years later, however, four justices appointed by President Nixon joined Justice Potter Stewart in limiting *Wade* and *Gilbert*. In *Kirby v. Illinois* (1972), the Court ruled that legal representation was required for lineups only when formal criminal charges had already been filed against a defendant.

have focused their investigation on that person, for example, telling police arriving at a murder scene, "I didn't mean to kill him." Police may also question someone who is not a suspect in a crime without giving the Miranda warning.

Although many law enforcement officials continued to view *Miranda* as an obstacle, the Miranda warning became part of standard police procedure. Officers adapted to "Mirandizing" suspects, and Miranda rights slowly became accepted in the law enforcement community. When the Supreme Court agreed to review *Withrow v. Williams*, a 1993 case involving Miranda issues, four police organizations and fifty former prosecutors filed a brief recommending that the Supreme Court preserve Miranda rights.

Despite all the protests that the *Miranda* ruling would reduce the number of confessions, some studies conducted since 1966 have consistently shown that Miranda warnings have had only a slight effect on confession rates. Law enforcement officials were surprised to discover that many suspects still agreed to talk, even after hearing Miranda warnings. Some suspects probably did not understand the warning; others may have felt genuine remorse over their crime or hoped that their confession would lead to a more lenient charge or sentence. Still others may have decided that they could talk their way out of trouble. Some police investigators also developed clever tactics to get around the *Miranda* ruling, such as making the Miranda warning seem unimportant or creating a delay in locating an attorney in hopes that the suspect would talk in the meantime.

REFINING MIRANDA RIGHTS

Later U.S. Supreme Court cases have reduced *Miranda*'s impact on law enforcement while supporting the decision's central ruling. In *Orozco v. Texas* (1969), the Court held that Miranda warnings were required even though police questioning took place in the defendant's home rather than a police station. Justice Byron White dissented, describing the *Miranda* ruling as a "constitutional straight jacket on law enforcement." In 1969, President Nixon appointed two new Supreme Court justices: Warren Burger (as chief justice) and Harry Blackmun. Both had publicly stated that they disagreed with the *Miranda* decision. Under Chief Justice Burger, the Court began chipping away at *Miranda*. In *Harris v. New York* (1971), the defendant had made statements before being read his Miranda rights. The Court held that although prosecutors could not use the defendant's statements as direct evidence, they could use the statements to challenge the truthfulness of the defendant's testimony at trial. In *Michigan v. Tucker* (1974), the police had informed the suspect that he had the right against self-incrimination, but they failed to inform him of his right to counsel. The suspect revealed the name of a witness, whose testimony helped convict the defendant. The Court held that although the defendant's statement itself could not be used as evidence, the witness identified in the statement could still testify against the defendant.

Over the years, the Supreme Court continued to refine its position on *Miranda*. In *Edwards v. Arizona* (1981), the defendant was arrested for robbery and murder. After being Mirandized, he requested to speak to an attorney, and the questioning ended. The next day, however, police officers questioned the defendant in jail once more, again informing him of his Miranda rights. During this second interrogation, the defendant waived his Miranda rights and confessed. The Court held that once a suspect has requested counsel, the police couldn't approach the suspect again to ask him to waive his Miranda rights.

In 2000, the Supreme Court considered *Dickerson v. United States*, which challenged the 1968 federal law that made voluntary statements admissible in federal criminal cases. The defendant had been charged with bank robbery and sought to prevent the prosecution from using a statement that he had made to the FBI before receiving the Miranda warning. The Supreme Court struck down the 1968 law, ruling that *Miranda* governs the admissibility of statements made during police interrogations in both state and federal courts. Speaking for the majority, Chief Justice William Rehnquist wrote, "This Court declines to overrule *Miranda* . . . [It] has become embedded in routine police practice to the point where the warnings have become part of our national culture." The majority opinion noted that Congress had enacted the statute to invalidate *Miranda*, but that Congress cannot override the Court's decisions interpreting and applying the Constitution.

In the most recent cases involving Miranda rights, the Court has given mixed signals. In *Missouri v. Seibert* (2004), the Court outlawed a police tactic known as "interrogating outside *Miranda*." In an attempt to get around *Miranda*, police had questioned a suspect before Mirandizing her. After getting the suspect to confess, they advised the suspect of her Miranda rights and then had her confess again. The Court ruled that this procedure violated the defendant's Miranda rights. In *United States v. Patane* (2004), the defendant interrupted the arresting officer in the middle of the Miranda warning, saying that he knew his rights. He then told the officer where to find a gun that he had hidden. The defendant sought to have the weapon excluded from his trial for illegal possession of a firearm. The Court ruled that the gun was admissible, holding that

Patrice Seibert is pictured here in an undated police file photo. The police did not Mirandize Seibert, hoping to get her to confess. After she confessed, the officers took a break and then read Seibert her Miranda rights, which she waived. They asked Seibert to repeat her confession, which she did. Seibert was convicted of second degree murder when her statements were used against her at her trial. In *Missouri v. Seibert* (2004), the U.S. Supreme Court ruled that this interrogation procedure violated her Miranda rights.

excluding evidence that resulted from a statement that occurred before the Miranda warning would be an unlawful extension of the *Miranda* ruling. Civil liberties advocates worried that the *Patane* ruling would encourage police to avoid Miranda rights in cases where they're more interested in finding crucial evidence than in obtaining a confession.

CHAPTER FOUR

The Future of Miranda Rights

As recent Supreme Court cases have shown, Miranda rights have become a vital part of the civil rights protections guaranteed to all U.S. citizens. Although the reach of the original decision has been limited by later cases, *Miranda*'s basic ruling–that the Fifth Amendment right against self-incrimination applies to police interrogations–remains intact. For nearly forty years, critics of the decision have been calling for the Supreme Court to reverse *Miranda*. During President Ronald Reagan's administration (1981–1989), the Justice Department even recommended abandoning *Miranda*. Encountering considerable criticism from civil rights groups and even from some law enforcement officials, it dropped the proposal. The *Miranda* ruling has survived constant criticism and still stands as the law of the land.

THE IMPORTANCE OF CONFESSIONS

Miranda settled the constitutional issue of whether the Fifth Amendment right against self-incrimination should apply to police interrogations. It also drew attention to an important public policy issue: what is the proper role of federal and state governments in obtaining confessions from citizens? Primarily because of the protections of the Bill of Rights, few other

Aaron Patterson *(left)* was falsely accused of murder and spent nearly seventeen years on death row. Illinois's governor pardoned Patterson in January 2003. Patterson is pictured here in June 2003 sitting behind the metal bench on which he scratched with a paper clip, "Aaron I lie about murders police threaten me with violence." Patterson alleged that Chicago police officers tortured him into falsely confessing to murder after they beat him and tried to suffocate him during interrogation.

Technology in the Interrogation Room

In response to concerns about the *Miranda* decision, some police departments began using audio recorders to tape suspects' confessions. Since camcorders became widely available in the mid-1980s, the videotaping of confessions has become a common procedure.

Taped confessions provide juries with a more objective record than written confessions of the interaction between police and a suspect during a confession. A Justice Department study in 2001 showed that 80 percent of police departments that videotaped confessions stated that videotaping helped them make their cases. The procedure of recording only confessions, however, still left room for unlawful pressure or abuse to occur *before* the confession was taped. Civil rights advocates argued that videotaping the entire interrogation process would deter police from using intimidating questioning methods. Critics of the videotaping of interrogations claimed that it would hinder investigators as they tried

On July 17, 2003, Illinois governor Rod Blagojevich signed a bill into law that requires the police to videotape interrogations and confessions in all homicide cases.

to get legal statements and that the cost was too high. Because of cost concerns, some police departments limit videotaping to murder investigations. Several states, however, require all interrogations to be videotaped.

countries rely on confessions to prove the guilt of a criminal defendant as much as the United States does. Law enforcement officials consider interrogations an essential part of their job. Obtaining confessions is a key goal because prosecutors like to build their cases around the defendant's admission of guilt. Confessions make it easier for prosecutors to get guilty verdicts and take criminals off the streets.

In any criminal investigation, the police have almost absolute control over interrogations. The pressures of police questioning have led some suspects to incriminate themselves when they were innocent. Such false confessions have resulted in erroneous convictions, which violates a principal belief of many Americans' sense of justice: that it's better to allow guilty parties to go free rather than to imprison an innocent person. Reliable confessions help assure a jury—and society—that the wrong person is not being punished.

MAINTAINING A BALANCE

Miranda proved so controversial because it tried to strike a difficult and delicate balance between two strongly opposing interests of American society. The Court sought to settle the conflict between the government's interest in promoting law enforcement and the interests of individuals in not having their constitutional rights violated. On one hand, law-abiding citizens rightly expect the government to control crime in their communities. On the other hand, the Constitution guarantees the independence and basic human dignity of all citizens. If courts place too many restrictions on law enforcement officers, they can make it more difficult for the police to solve crimes. If courts remove restraints on police conduct, they may increase the likelihood that the fundamental rights of suspects will be abused.

The ultimate aim of the Miranda warning is to balance the freedom of suspects to make up their own minds against society's need to allow police to seek confessions from suspects whom they believe are guilty. Because of legislative responses to citizen complaints

This police interrogation was videotaped in San Diego, California, on February 5, 2002. Several states, including Illinois, Minnesota, and Alaska, require police interrogations to be videotaped. By being required to record interrogations and confessions, those in law enforcement will be less likely to abuse a suspect's rights and more likely to make their cases hold up in court.

about crime control, criminal procedures in the United States tend to tilt in the favor of law enforcement. In *Miranda*, the Supreme Court pointed out that coercion is always present during police interrogations. Allowing suspects access to legal counsel helps even out the unfair advantage held by law enforcement. "With a lawyer present," the Court wrote, "the likelihood that the police will practice coercion is reduced, and if coercion is nevertheless exercised the lawyer can testify to it in court. The presence of a lawyer can also help to guarantee that the accused gives a fully accurate statement to the police and that the statement is rightly reported by the prosecution at trial." The *Miranda* ruling provides suspects with the option to remain silent when questioned by police. If they choose to talk, they may request to face the interrogation with an expert on their side— one who is interested in protecting their rights.

MIRANDA'S LEGACY

Miranda warnings have not solved all the problems that might occur with police interrogations. Current cases involving confessions often raise the issue of whether suspects waived their rights knowingly and voluntarily. It's not always easy for courts to decide whether the suspect understood the Miranda warning and freely chose to speak to police interrogators. Some civil rights advocates have argued that *Miranda* has merely encouraged police to use less obvious means to pressure or trick suspects into making statements.

The *Miranda* decision attempted to make clear the government's role in obtaining confessions. It sought to establish a consistent understanding of a criminal defendant's rights and aimed to end the use of violence and physical intimidation to wring confessions out of a suspect. Most important, it reaffirmed the Constitution's guarantees that "[n]o person . . . shall be compelled in any criminal case to be a witness against himself," and that "the accused shall . . . have the Assistance of Counsel."

Most legal scholars consider *Miranda* to be the most controversial criminal procedure case that the U.S. Supreme Court has ever decided. Many Americans view its ultimate aim, to protect the accused from unfair pressures during police questioning, as over-protecting criminals. In balancing the competing interests of law enforcement and individual rights, the Court created a procedure that lessened the risks suspects faced during interrogations. By requiring police to inform suspects of their Fifth Amendment right to remain silent and their Sixth Amendment right to counsel before questioning, the Court has provided the accused with greater protections. The

Miranda warning is important because it helps ensure the reliability of confessions. As the Supreme Court noted in *Withrow v. Williams*, "*Miranda* facilitates the correct ascertainment of guilt by guarding against the use of unreliable statements at trial." Fair trials ensure justice in individual cases, maintain public confidence in criminal verdicts, and promote faith in the U.S. judicial system.

GLOSSARY

appeal A request for a review by a higher court of a law case previously decided in a lower court.

arraignment A legal proceeding during which an accused person is brought before a court to answer a charge.

brief A document submitted to the court by a lawyer (or other party) that outlines the legal arguments in a case.

confession A voluntary statement by an accused person that he or she has committed a crime.

criminal procedure Legal methods used in the capture, trial, and punishment of a person accused of breaking the law.

cross-examination Questioning of a witness in a court case by the lawyer on the opposing side.

felony A major crime, such as robbery or murder, that may be punishable by confinement in a state or federal prison.

immunity A privilege granted to a person that exempts that person from prosecution for any self-incriminating testimony given before a court, a grand jury, or an investigating committee.

inadmissible Not allowed to be presented as evidence in a court of law.

interrogation Questioning of a suspect or a witness by police or other law enforcement officials.

justice A judge, particularly one of the nine judges of the U.S. Supreme Court.

landmark case A case of such importance that it establishes new law.

lineup A group of people, standing in line, from which police ask a crime witness to identify the guilty party.

Mirandize To read Miranda warnings to a criminal suspect.

overrule To reverse a decision made in a lower court.

prosecutor Lawyer who represents the government in a trial.

rape Unlawful sexual intercourse carried out forcibly or under threat of injury against the will of the victim.

self-incrimination Giving testimony against oneself.

Supreme Court The highest court in the United States, the decisions of which are binding on all other courts in the country, the federal government, and state governments.

unconstitutional In violation of the principles set out in the U.S. Constitution.

verdict The decision by a jury (or, in some cases, a judge) at the end of a trial.

waiver The voluntary giving up of a right or benefit.

FOR MORE INFORMATION

National District Attorneys Association
99 Canal Center Plaza, Suite 510
Alexandria, VA 22314
(703) 549-9222
Web site: http://www.ndaa.org

National Legal Aid & Defender Association
1140 Connecticut Avenue NW, Suite 900
Washington, DC 20036
(202) 452-0620
Web site: http://www.nlada.org

Supreme Court Historical Society
Opperman House
224 East Capitol Street NE
Washington, DC 20543
(202) 543-0400
Web site: http://www.supremecourtus.gov

Web Sites

Due to the changing nature of Internet links, the Rosen Publishing Group, Inc., has developed an online list of Web sites related to the subject of this book. This site is updated regularly. Please use this link to access the list:

http://www.rosenlinks.com/lallp/miri

FOR FURTHER READING

Banaszak, Ronald Sr. *Fair Trial Rights of the Accused: A Documentary History.* Westport, CT: Greenwood, 2002.

Gold, Susan Dudley. *Miranda v. Arizona: Suspects' Rights.* New York, NY: Twenty-First Century Books, 1997.

Patrick, John J. *The Bill of Rights: A History in Documents.* New York, NY: Oxford University Press, 2003.

Quiri, Patricia Ryon. *The Bill of Rights.* New York, NY: Children's Press, 1998.

Riley, Gail Blasser. *Miranda v. Arizona: Rights of the Accused.* Springfield, NJ: Enslow, 1994.

Sonneborn, Liz. *Miranda v. Arizona: The Rights of the Accused.* (Supreme Court Cases Through Primary Sources). New York, NY: Rosen Publishing Group, 2004.

Wice, Paul. *Gideon v. Wainright and the Right to Counsel.* Danbury, CT: Franklin Watts, 1995.

Wice, Paul. *Miranda v. Arizona: "You Have the Right to Remain Silent . . ."* Danbury, CT: Franklin Watts, 1996.

BIBLIOGRAPHY

Baker, Liva. *Miranda: Crime, Law, and Politics.* New York, NY: Atheneum, 1985.

Banaszak, Ronald Sr. *Fair Trial Rights of the Accused: A Documentary History.* Westport, CT: Greenwood, 2002.

Barker, Lucius, et al. *Civil Liberties and the Constitution.* 9th ed. Englewood Cliffs, NJ: Prentice Hall, 2004.

Findlaw U.S. Supreme Court Opinions. "*Miranda v. Arizona* (1966)." Retrieved August 18, 2004 (http://caselaw.lp.findlaw.com/ scripts/getcase.pl?court=us&vol=384&invol=436).

Hoffman, Ronald, and Peter J. Albert, eds. *Bill of Rights: Government Proscribed.* Charlottesville, VA: University of Virginia Press, 1998.

Leo, Richard A. et al., eds. *The Miranda Debate: Law, Justice, and Policing.* Boston, MA: Northeastern University Press, 1998.

Markon, Jerry. "Police Tactic to Sidestep Miranda Rights Rejected." *Washington Post,* June 29, 2004, p. 1.

Nowak, John E., and Ronald D. Rotunda. *Constitutional Law.* (Hornbook Series). 7th ed. Eagan, MN: West Group, 2004.

White, Welch S. *Miranda's Waning Protections.* Ann Arbor, MI: University of Michigan Press, 2001.

INDEX

About the Author

G. S. Prentzas, a writer and editor living in New York, has written eleven books for young readers, including a biography of Thurgood Marshall and a book on traditional Native American law. He graduated with honors from the University of North Carolina School of Law.

Photo Credits

Cover, p. 1 © Royalty Free/Corbis; p. 5 © Bob Daemmrich /The Image Works; pp. 7, 9, 10 Arizona State Library, Archives and Public Records, Archives Division, Phoenix; p. 8 Courtesy Carroll Cooley; pp. 13, 26, 27 © Bettmann/Corbis; p. 14 © The *New York Times*; p. 18 HIP/Scala/Art Resource, NY; p. 19 © Virginia Museum of Fine Arts, Richmond. Gift of Edgar William and Bernice Chrysler Garbisch. Photo Ron Jennings; p. 20 National Archives; p. 23 © Art Shay/Time Life Pictures/Getty Images; p. 32 © Missouri Department of Corrections/AP/Wide World Photos; p. 35 © Stephen J. Carrera/AP/Wide World Photos; p. 36 © M. Spencer Green/AP/Wide World Photos; p. 38 © CNN/Getty Images.

Designer: Thomas Forget; Editor: Kathy Kuhtz Campbell
Photo Researcher: Amy Feinberg